Francis Frith's

North and East Hertfordshire

Photographic Memories

Francis Frith's North and East Hertfordshire

Tom Doig

First published in the United Kingdom in 2002 by
Frith Book Company Ltd

Hardback Edition 2002
ISBN 1-85937-547-2

British Library Cataloguing in Publication Data

Francis Frith's North and East Hertfordshire
Tom Doig

Frith Book Company Ltd
Frith's Barn, Teffont,
Salisbury, Wiltshire SP3 5QP
Tel: +44 (0) 1722 716 376
Email: info@francisfrith.co.uk
www.francisfrith.co.uk

Printed and bound in Great Britain

Front Cover: **Bishop's Stortford, General View 1899** 44282

AS WITH ANY HISTORICAL DATABASE THE FRITH ARCHIVE IS CONSTANTLY BEING CORRECTED AND IMPROVED AND THE PUBLISHERS WOULD WELCOME INFORMATION ON OMISSIONS OR INACCURACIES

Contents

Francis Frith: *Victorian Pioneer*

Francis Frith, Victorian founder of the world-famous photographic archive, was a complex and multi-talented man. A devout Quaker and a highly successful Victorian businessman, he was both philosophic by nature and pioneering in outlook.

By 1855 Francis Frith had already established a wholesale grocery business in Liverpool, and sold it for the astonishing sum of £200,000, which is the equivalent today of over £15,000,000. Now a multi-millionaire, he was able to indulge his passion for travel. As a child he had pored over travel books written by early explorers, and his fancy and imagination had been stirred by family holidays to the sublime mountain regions of Wales and Scotland. 'What a land of spirit-stirring and enriching scenes and places!' he had written. He was to return to these scenes of grandeur in later years to 'recapture the thousands of vivid and tender memories', but with a different purpose. Now in his thirties, and captivated by the new science of photography, Frith set out on a series of pioneering journeys to the Nile regions that occupied him from 1856 until 1860.

Intrigue and Adventure

He took with him on his travels a specially-designed wicker carriage that acted as both dark-room and sleeping chamber. These far-flung journeys were packed with intrigue and adventure. In his life story, written when he was sixty-three, Frith tells of being held captive by bandits, and of fighting 'an awful midnight battle to the very point of surrender with a deadly pack of hungry, wild dogs'. Sporting flowing Arab costume, Frith arrived at Akaba by camel seventy years before Lawrence, where he encountered 'desert princes and rival sheikhs, blazing with jewel-hilted swords'.

During these extraordinary adventures he was assiduously exploring the desert regions bordering the Nile and patiently recording the antiquities and peoples with his camera. He was the first photographer to venture beyond the sixth cataract. Africa was still the mysterious 'Dark Continent', and Stanley and Livingstone's historic meeting was a decade into the future. The conditions for picture taking confound belief. He laboured for hours in his wicker dark-room in the sweltering heat of the desert, while the volatile chemicals fizzed dangerously in their trays. Often he was forced to work in remote tombs and caves where conditions were cooler. Back in London he exhibited his photographs and was 'rapturously cheered' by members of the Royal Society. His reputation as a photographer was made overnight. An eminent modern historian has likened their impact on the population of the time to that on our own generation of the first photographs taken on the surface of the moon.

Venture of a Life-Time

Characteristically, Frith quickly spotted the opportunity to create a new business as a specialist publisher of photographs. He lived in an era of immense and sometimes violent change. For the poor in the early part of Victoria's reign work was a drudge and the hours long, and people had precious little free time to enjoy themselves. Most had no transport other than a cart or gig at their disposal, and had not travelled far beyond the boundaries of their own town or village. However, by the 1870s, the railways had threaded their way across the country, and Bank Holidays and half-day Saturdays had been made obligatory by Act of Parliament. All of a sudden the ordinary working man and his family were able to enjoy days out and see a little more of the world.

With characteristic business acumen, Francis Frith foresaw that these new tourists would enjoy having souvenirs to commemorate their days out. In 1860 he married Mary Ann Rosling and set out with the intention of photographing every city, town and village in Britain. For the next thirty years he travelled the country by train and by pony and trap, producing fine photographs of seaside resorts and beauty spots that were keenly bought by millions of Victorians. These prints were painstakingly pasted into family albums and pored over during the dark nights of winter, rekindling precious memories of summer excursions.

The Rise of Frith & Co

Frith's studio was soon supplying retail shops all over the country. To meet the demand he gathered about him a small team of photographers, and published the work of independent artist-photographers of the calibre of Roger Fenton and Francis Bedford. In order to gain some understanding of the scale of Frith's business one only has to look at the catalogue issued by Frith & Co in 1886: it runs to some 670 pages, listing not only many thousands of views of the British Isles but also many photographs of most European countries, and China, Japan, the USA and Canada – note the sample page shown above from the hand-written *Frith & Co* ledgers detailing pictures taken. By 1890 Frith had created the greatest specialist photographic publishing company in the world,

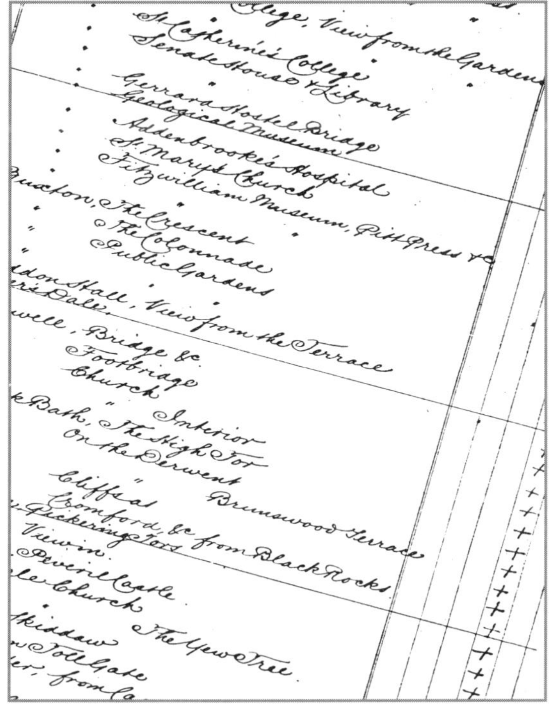

ollege, View from the Gardens
St Catherine's College
Senate House & Library
Gerrard Hostel Bridge
Geological Museum
Addenbrooke's Hospital
St Mary's Church
Fitzwilliam Museum, Pitt Press &c
uxton, The Crescent
The Colonnade
Public Gardens
ddon Hall, View from the Terrace
rs Dale.
well, Bridge &c.
Footbridge
Church
" Interior
k Bath, " The High Tor
On the Derwent
" Brunswood Terrace
Cliffe at
Cromford, &c from Black Rocks
Pickering Tor
View in
Peveril Castle
le Church
The Yew Tree.
kiddaw
Toll Gate
er, from Co

with over 2,000 outlets – more than the combined number that Boots and WH Smith have today! The picture on the right shows the *Frith & Co* display board at Ingleton in the Yorkshire Dales. Beautifully constructed with mahogany frame and gilt inserts, it could display up to a dozen local scenes.

Postcard Bonanza

The ever-popular holiday postcard we know today took many years to develop. In 1870 the Post Office issued the first plain cards, with a pre-printed stamp on one face. In 1894 they allowed other publishers' cards to be sent through the mail with an attached adhesive halfpenny stamp. Demand grew rapidly, and in 1895 a new size of postcard was permitted called the court card, but there was little room for illustration. In 1899, a year after Frith's death, a new card measuring 5.5 x 3.5 inches became the standard format, but it was not until 1902 that the divided back came into being, with address and message on one face and a full-size illustration on the other. *Frith & Co* were in the vanguard of postcard development, and Frith's sons Eustace and Cyril continued their father's monumental task, expanding the number of views offered to the public and recording more and more places in Britain, as the coasts and countryside were opened up to mass travel.

Francis Frith died in 1898 at his villa in Cannes, his great project still growing. The archive he created continued in business for another seventy years. By 1970 it contained over a third of a million pictures of 7,000 cities, towns and villages. The massive photographic record Frith has left to us stands as a living monument to a special and very remarkable man.

Frith's Archive: *A Unique Legacy*

Francis Frith's legacy to us today is of immense significance and value, for the magnificent archive of evocative photographs he created provides a unique record of change in 7,000 cities, towns and villages throughout Britain over a century and more. Frith and his fellow studio photographers revisited locations many times down the years to update their views, compiling for us an enthralling and colourful pageant of British life and character.

We tend to think of Frith's sepia views of Britain as nostalgic, for most of us use them to conjure up memories of places in our own lives with which we have family associations. It often makes us forget that to Francis Frith they were records of daily life as it was actually being lived in the cities, towns and villages of his day. The Victorian age was one of great and often bewildering change for ordinary people, and though the pictures evoke an impression of slower times, life was as busy and hectic as it is today.

See Frith at www.francisfrith.co.uk

We are fortunate that Frith was a photographer of the people, dedicated to recording the minutiae of everyday life. For it is this sheer wealth of visual data, the painstaking chronicle of changes in dress, transport, street layouts, buildings, housing, engineering and landscape that captivates us so much today. His remarkable images offer us a powerful link with the past and with the lives of our ancestors.

Today's Technology

Computers have now made it possible for Frith's many thousands of images to be accessed almost instantly. In the Frith archive today, each photograph is carefully 'digitised' then stored on a CD Rom. Frith archivists can locate a single photograph amongst thousands within seconds. Views can be catalogued and sorted under a variety of categories of place and content to the immediate benefit of researchers.

Inexpensive reference prints can be created for them at the touch of a mouse button, and a wide range of books and other printed materials assembled and published for a wider, more general readership - in the next twelve months over a hundred Frith local history titles will be published! The day-to-day workings of the archive are very different from how they were in Francis Frith's time: imagine the herculean task of sorting through eleven tons of glass negatives as Frith had to do to locate a particular sequence of pictures! Yet the archive still prides itself on maintaining the same high standards of excellence laid down by Francis Frith, including the painstaking cataloguing and indexing of every view.

It is curious to reflect on how the internet now allows researchers in America and elsewhere greater instant access to the archive than Frith himself ever enjoyed. Many thousands of individual views can be called up on screen within seconds on one of the Frith internet sites, enabling people living continents away to revisit the streets of their ancestral home town, or view places in Britain where they have enjoyed holidays. Many overseas researchers welcome the chance to view special theme selections, such as transport, sports, costume and ancient monuments.

We are certain that Francis Frith would have heartily approved of these modern developments in imaging techniques, for he himself was always working at the very limits of Victorian photographic technology.

The Value of the Archive Today

Because of the benefits brought by the computer, Frith's images are increasingly studied by social historians, by researchers into genealogy and ancestory, by architects, town planners, and by teachers and schoolchildren involved in local history projects.

In addition, the archive offers every one of us an opportunity to examine the places where we and our families have lived and worked down the years. Highly successful in Frith's own era, the archive is now, a century and more on, entering a new phase of popularity.

The Past in Tune with the Future

Historians consider the Francis Frith Collection to be of prime national importance. It is the only archive of its kind remaining in private ownership and has been valued at a million pounds. However, this figure is now rapidly increasing as digital technology enables more and more people around the world to enjoy its benefits.

Francis Frith's archive is now housed in an historic timber barn in the beautiful village of Teffont in Wiltshire. Its founder would not recognize the archive office as it is today. In place of the many thousands of dusty boxes containing glass plate negatives and an all-pervading odour of photographic chemicals, there are now ranks of computer screens. He would be amazed to watch his images travelling round the world at unimaginable speeds through network and internet lines.

The archive's future is both bright and exciting. Francis Frith, with his unshakeable belief in making photographs available to the greatest number of people, would undoubtedly approve of what is being done today with his lifetime's work. His photographs, depicting our shared past, are now bringing pleasure and enlightenment to millions around the world a century and more after his death.

North and East Hertfordshire
An Introduction

MANY MOTORISTS DRIVING along the northern Hertfordshire border do not realise that they are following a route taken by our ancestors from the earliest times. The Icknield Way follows the northern scarp of the eastern end of the Chilterns and passes close to Ickleton in the west and Ickleford, in Essex, in the east. This pre-Iron Age track connects a series of towns and villages like a string of pearls. It was not, however, a single defined track, but rather a series of parallel paths running cross-country. Our photographs illustrate many of these communities - Lilley, Ickleford, Hitchin, Baldock, Royston on the main Icknield Way, with many villages on the parallel tracks such as Norton and Ashwell (on the northern Ashwell Strete) and Charlton, Barkway and Barley on the southern trackways. The favoured route varied with the weather, for the lower, and more northern tracks would become waterlogged in winter, whilst the higher routes were dry and could not provide water for flocks of sheep and droves of cattle.

In time, many of these villages developed into towns, particularly at places where the Icknield Way crossed the later Roman Roads. It is said that Baldock was founded around 1140 by the Knights Templar at a point where the Icknield Way was crossed by Roman roads from Braughing and Verulamium (St Albans), whilst Royston sprang up at the crossing with Ermine Street. The Canons of St Rohesias at the Cross were awarded a market in

1189, but it was not until 1897 that Royston became a town in its own right. Until then it was split, like segments of an orange, by five parishes - three in Cambridgeshire and two in Hertfordshire.

It was not only at the crossings that settlements developed. The name of the village of Chipping, to the north of Buntingford, records an abortive attempt in 1252 to establish a market on the pre-Roman Ermine Street. Chipping is an early word for market, and appears in many towns across the country - Chipping Barnet, Chipping Campden, Chipping Sodbury and many others. Buntingford (or Layston as it was originally called) developed at a crossing place through the River Rib, and succeeded where Chipping failed. Its market charter is dated 1360. Of the villages illustrated, Hitchin, Baldock, Ashwell, Royston, Barkway, Buntingford, Westmill, Standon, Bishop's Stortford, Ware, Sawbridgeworth, Hertford and Stanstead all enjoyed market charters and many had pie powder courts. The name is derived from the French 'pieds poudrés', the powdery or dusty feet of the travellers gathering at the market. These courts were empowered to give summary justice to pickpockets, false weight swindlers, sleight of hand magicians, and so on without recourse to the county courts.

Most of these communities along the Icknield Way are served by rivers and streams (such as the Hiz, the Rhee, the Houghton and the Pirral) which drain northwards into the Cam and the Ouse and eventually to the Wash. On the south side of the Chilterns, rivers such as the Lea, the Mimram, the Beane, the Rib (or Quin), the Ash and the Stort drain into the Thames. On these south-bound rivers stand the settlements in east Hertfordshire. They developed into towns such as Buntingford, Ware, Hertford, Stortford and Sawbridgeworth and villages like Much Hadham, Hunsdon and Wareside.

Much of the improvement of rivers into canals came in the west of the county in the mid 1700s. However, in 1609, Sir Hugh Middleton proposed the construction of an aqueduct to provide fresh water from Amwell Spring, just south of Ware, to London. The Lee Navigation, in all its forms, provided fresh water and a direct water-borne access to London. By the end of the 18th century, it is said, 5,000 quarters of malt were being carried from Ware to London each week. The ballast on the narrow boats coming back to Hertfordshire was household waste and human and animal manure, which was used to fertilize the 'fruitfull fieldes of pleasant Hertfordshire', as William Vallens put it in his 'The Tale of Two Swannes' in 1589. Along with straw plaiting, silk weaving, brewing and paper making, the production of malt was a major industry in Hertfordshire, and contributed to its prosperity. Queen Elizabeth I had called Hertfordshire the malt basket of her kingdom and 'would often boast of her Hitchen grape.'

In December 1588, John Nicholls was granted a

six-month licence to dig in Hertfordshire for 'mynes or myneralls of golde, silver, tynne or leade, hidden in the earth'. What Nicholls forgot was that Hertfordshire's gold would not be found below ground. It shows itself above ground in late summer and early autumn. Needless to say, the licence was not renewed!

John Edwin Cussans, writing in 1873, reminds us that 'the nursery gardens of Hertfordshire should not be forgotten: those of Messrs Paul of Cheshunt and Waltham, and Messrs Rivers of Sawbridgeworth, deserve special notice'. The rich soil of the flood plain of the River Lea encouraged the growth of a nursery industry which, in time became, one of the most prosperous in Europe.

The main problem with the canal trade was that every time a waterway arrived at a hill, a tunnel or a series of locks was necessary. Vallens, in his 'Tale of Two Swannes', tells us as early as 1589 of '... the locke through which the boats of Ware do passe with malt. This locke containes two double doors of wood, within the same cesterne all of planke, which onely fils when boates come there to pass by opening of these mightie dors ...'

As early as the beginning of the 1700s, it was clear that traditional roads would provide a better communication system, and a network of turnpikes, essentially toll roads, was set up. In the main, these followed the course of the old Roman roads. The Wadesmill Turnpike was initially established in 1663 and reinstated in 1733, and went from Ware to Royston and on to Huntingdon, with a branch at Braughing towards Cambridge; the Icknield Way Turnpike of 1769 went from Luton via Hitchin and Baldock to Royston; the Cheshunt Turnpike of 1725 went from Enfield to Hertford and Ware; and the Hockerill Turnpike of 1744 linked Harlow, Sawbridgeworth and Bishops Stortford. Today, the old Wadesmill Turnpike is followed by the course of the A10 (with a branch at Braughing along the B1368 through Barkway and Barley); the Cheshunt Turnpike has become the southern part of the A10; the Icknield Turnpike is now the A505 and the Hockerill Turnpike has become the A1184 and the M11. Clearly, the turnpike network stood the test of time.

Much of the work on the building, maintenance and improvement of the turnpike system in Hertfordshire was the work of the famous John Loudon McAdam (known as the Colossus of Roads) and his son James, who lived in Hoddesdon High Street. Their method of establishing a hard and durable road surface made from a matrix of crushed stones offered employment for the labouring people of the county, and provided a useful disposal for the stones picked from the fields by the older ladies in the village communities. Many of the roads in north and east Hertfordshire are, even today, built on the base manufactured by the McAdams.

The arrival of the railways signalled a death blow to the turnpike trusts - they were dissolved in 1862. The first lines to be built in Hertfordshire were at Watford and Tring. By 1842 the eastern part of the county was serviced by a line from London through Waltham Cross (branching to Stanstead Abbots) and Harlow, in Essex, northwards to Sawbridgeworth and Bishops Stortford towards Cambridge. The particularly picturesque Buntingford branch line served Ware, Wareside (at Mardock), Much Hadham, Standon, Braughing, Westmill and, finally, Buntingford. All of these places are featured in Frith's photographs. One wonders if the Frith photographers travelled on the line! Across the north of Hertfordshire, the line from Hitchin via Letchworth (where the station was built in 1903), Baldock, Ashwell, Royston and on to Cambridge opened in 1850. Despite a number of abortive proposals, no line up the eastern side of the county to Royston was ever constructed, and those villages and markets which had flourished during the time of the turnpikes withered and became quiet rural backwaters.

The railways brought new opportunities, new materials, and new aspirations. Many villagers in the north and east of Hertfordshire had rarely been beyond their villages in their lives - it was just an occasional annual treat to visit the local town on market or fair day. Suddenly they were able to visit the great cities. The railhead was attainable to all but the remotest communities, and many a village society or public house organised trips to London to see the Great Exhibition of 1851. Country folk were astounded at what they saw, and brought back tales of rows of stone houses and busy streets where everything that the heart could desire was available for purchase. Within a few years, the Sunday Schools had abandoned wagon rides for their treats - a railway trip to the seaside at Hunstanton or Cromer was the order of the day. The staff of the Hertfordshire Mercury and the Royston Crow took their annual wazygoose at Newmarket or Southend.

During the 20th century, north and east Hertfordshire in the main avoided the development of new towns. These were generally confined to the area bordering the Great North Road in central and southern Hertfordshire. Hatfield New Town, Welwyn Garden City and Stevenage, along the A1 corridor, welcomed the London overspill, and so did Hemel Hempstead in the west. On the border with Bedfordshire, under the guidance of Ebenezer Howard, Letchworth provided a ground-breaking new direction in town development. Howard's Garden City Company, formed in 1903, forged a template for future urban development, and has been hailed as one of the major steps forward in social progress in the modern era. Of course, many towns (and some villages) have expanded with new housing complexes and industrial estates. In the 1970s, the furthest north-east corner of the county,

at Nuthampstead, narrowly missed becoming the hub of the 'third London airport'; Stanstead, in Essex, gained this dubious honour.

The routes followed by Frith's photographers take today's traveller through quiet villages, bustling market towns, winding rivers and abandoned canals. Fifty or so years ago, the roads were quieter and the canals still busy with traffic, but the markets still bustled and the villages were still quiet.

The habitués of the markets and their inns and public houses comprised, as a document in the British Museum says of Hertford, 'all persons calling themselves Scholars, going about begging, all Sea-faring men, pretending losses of the ships and goods at sea; all idle persons going about the county, begging or using any subtle craft, or unlawful Games, Players, or feigning themselves to have knowledge in Physiognomy, Palmistry, or other like crafty services, pretending that they can tell destinies, fortunes, or such other phantastical imaginations. All collectors for Gaols, Prisons or Hospitals; all Fencers, Bearwards, common players of Interludes and Minstrels: all Juglers, Tinkers, Pedlars, Petty Chapmen wandering abroad, and Ballad singers; all wandering persons and Common Labourers, using loytering, and refusing to work for such reasonable wages as taxed ... All persons, not being felons, pretending to Egyptians, or wandering in the form, habit or attire of counterfeit Egyptians; and all such persons as wander up and down the county to sell Glasses, etc'. They were experts at 'swearing, drunkeness, suffering disorders, tippling, gaming, or playing at Tables, Billiard-Table, Shovel-board, Cards, Dice, Nine-pins, Pigeon-holes, Trunks ... Bowling-Alley or Bowling-Green'.

The population now is a different, more cosmopolitan society - the Hertfordshire accent surfaces only occasionally on market days. Sawbridgeworth is still known locally as Sapsford, Hoddesdon as Hodsdon, Nuthampstead as Nutsted, Aspenden as Aspden and Hertford as Harford - just leave out the middle syllable and you will be accepted as a local! But beware the pitfalls of Braughing - call it anything else other than 'Braffing' and you will be laughed out of town.

Children from many other countries and religions integrate into Hertfordshire's much envied education system, and the younger ones are increasingly aware of their status in a unified Europe. But we may be glad that they continue our traditions - they dance round the maypole, they applaud the morris dance, they make corn dollies and, most important of all, they pronounce the names of the villages correctly.

The people of north and east Hertfordshire jealously guard their rural heritage, but at the same time they look forward to a prosperous future for their children. Some inhabitants are unaware of the changes which have taken place in the county. Francis Frith's photographers have made sure that the style of life in the 1900s will not be forgotten. If we follow their trail, we will enjoy the unrecognised charm of this part of rural Hertfordshire. But we must keep our eyes peeled for 'Fencers, Bearwards, Juglers, Tinkers, Pedlers and Ballad Singers'.

Lilley
The Lilley Arms c1955 L506001

The Lilley Arms is the oldest public house in the village and dates from around 1705. Originally called the Sugar Loaf, in 1852 its name was changed to the Sowerby Arms out of respect to the lord of the manor. During the Great War, it changed again to the Lilley Arms. For many years the adjacent building was occupied by the village blacksmith. Lilley was the home of Johan Kellerman, a famous alchemist who boasted that he could change mercury into gold. It is said that he lived in squalor in one room protected by sliding bolts and patent padlocks. Kellerman boasted that 'the world, sir, is in my hands and my power'. Eventually he was chased away and died in poverty in Paris.

Whitwell, High Street c1955 W175017d
The tranquil village of Whitwell lies directly under the flightpath of aircraft landing at Luton Airport. The earliest mention of the Bull public house, on the left, is in 1675, although the building is much earlier. In the 1830s, the Bull's sign spanned the High Street, but this was removed after a number of accidents in other parts of the county. The Bull provided food and accommodation as well as beer. In 1808 a diarist wrote that he attended an expensive dinner where twenty people consumed beef, chicken, ham, goose, duck and pie for 15s per head. An attractive village, Whitwell was home to Alan Sillitoe, the novelist, Robert Newton, the actor and Sir Francis Camps, the forensic pathologist.

St Paul's Walden All Saints' Church c1950
S761013
A Morris 8 Series E waits patiently outside the church of All Saints in the village of Whitwell, which, with Bendish, forms the parish of St Paul's Walden. Two traditional occupations - straw plaiting and watercress cultivation - provided an income for the inhabitants. Stagenhoe Park to the north-east of the villages was the home of Sir Arthur Sullivan.

Whitwell, Horn Hill c1955 W175017e
Whitwell was home to two special industries - straw plaiting and watercress production. The Plaiting School in the village employed village ladies and children who supplemented the low agricultural wages by weaving strips of straw, called plait, to the hat-making trade in Luton. To the west of the village are the Nine Wells, the source of the River Mimram. The wetlands provide ideal conditions for growing watercress; Whitwell watercress was in great demand in London, where it was sold for 1/2d per bunch. Horn Hill leads from Whitwell south-westwards to Kimpton.

Charlton, Brick Kiln Lane 1903
49746
The village of Charlton lies about 3/4 mile to the south-west of Hitchin. At the time of Domesday it was held by King William himself - before 1066, it was included in Earl Harold's estates as part of Hitchin. The River Hiz has its source just south of the village, and a watermill is recorded in the village in Domesday. In the 1800s, the villagers' income came from the straw-plaiting industry, which served the hat-making trade at Luton. Sir Henry Bessemer, the inventor of the Bessemer conversion process for manufacturing steel, was born here. It is said that Dog Kennel Farm, at Charlton, was originally kennels for Henry VIII's hunting hounds.

Ickleford, The Village 1903 49749

Two miles north of Hitchin lies Ickleford, where the Roman Icknield way crosses the confluence of the Rivers Hiz and Oughton. The bridge was built to replace the ford in the early part of the 19th century. It is said that the abbot of St Albans held his local court in an upper room of the George Inn next to the parish church of St Katherine.

Ickleford, The Fields 1903 49750

This view probably shows the fields and open ground at Lower Green, north of Ickleford and close to the Bedfordshire border. John Edwin Cussans, writing at the end of the 19th century, says that two miles north of Ickleford, Meppleshall was a detached part of Hertfordshire entirely surrounded by Bedfordshire. The county boundary cuts through the parlour of the old rectory, and an old oak beam in the fireplace was carved with the words: 'If you wish to go into Hertfordshire, Hitch in a little nearer the fire'.

Hitchin, The Priory 1901 46654

The Priory stands on the banks of the River Hiz (from which the town of Hitchin gets its name), and dates back to the time of King Edward II. He granted a small portion of Hitchin to the White Friars or Carmelites who built the original priory. In 1539 they were forced to surrender it to the king, and it was eventually passed to the Radcliffe family, whose descendants continued to hold it until the 19th century.

Hitchin, Priory Park 1901 46651

Bounded by Gosmoor and Charlton Roads, Priory Park was a favourite spot for picnics and Sunday afternoon strolls down to the banks of the River Hiz close to Brick Kiln Lane, Charlton, which runs behind the trees on the right of the picture. The Victorian children are picking daises to make daisy chains, unaware of the tall ghostly lady wearing a red cloak and black hat who was seen walking across the park by Richard Atkins, a local butcher, in 1816.

Hitchin, The Biggin 1903
49742
The Biggin was originally built in 1361 by Sir Edward de Kendale as a Gilbertine priory. The priory was dissolved in 1538, and it became a residence. Later it was used as a school, and formed part of the workhouse and poorhouse for the town. It now provides accommodation as almshouses.

SPRATTS
DOG CAKES

Hitchin, Walsworth Road 1922 71895
Walsworth Road runs from the railway station to the centre of Hitchin. We might be forgiven for believing that this is a quiet backwater in a developing market town. Today it is a busy commuter route, but in 1922 children could play on the street, and the traffic offered very little respect to the rules of the road.

COCK HOTEL

Hitchin, High Street 1929 81713
The photographer stood with his back to the market place looking towards Bancroft. On the left is the Cock Inn - it was given its name from the cockpit at the rear. The Cock Inn was once a tumbledown, disreputable place, but Alfred Doughty's obituary in 1916 says that after he purchased the inn in 1888, he improved it, 'until today The Cock Inn is one of the finest houses in the county'.

H.M.BAINS

Hitchin, Hermitage Road 1929 81722
Hermitage Road was opened in 1875 to give the people of Hitchin better access to the railway station. The land was given by Frederick Seebohm, who owned the Hermitage Estate. The fine avenue of box trees was removed - box wood was in great demand by the Luton hat makers for use as blocking moulds - and houses and shops were built. The area on the far right of the road formed the rear of Portmill Lane, which had been cleared in preparation for development; its residents were re-housed on the Sunnyside Estate.

Hitchin, Windmill Hill 1922 71981

In 1875, Mr Tuke's windmill caught fire. Isaac Chalkley, Superintendent of the Hitchin Fire Brigade, brought the new horse-drawn Shand-Mason pump to the site, and the fire appeared to be under control. Suddenly it flared up again, and despite the efforts of the brigade, all was in vain and the mill was destroyed. From this favourite picnic spot, we can see the parish church standing proudly in the centre of the picture with the trees to its right covering the new market and car parks.

Hitchin, The William Ransom Buildings, Bancroft 1931 84206
The Ransoms were a strong Quaker family with wide-ranging contacts in many fields. William Ransom, born in 1826 in the house at the north end of Bancroft, studied at Isaac Brown's Quaker Academy at the Triangle, Hitchin. Whilst at Isaac Brown's he met Joseph Lister (after whom the Lister Hospital is named), Birket Foster, the watercolour painter, and Joseph Pollard, the famous botanist. Ransom set up a successful pharmaceutical business, and was well-known for his antiquarian pursuits.

Hitchin, Bridge Street c1955 H89012
The Plough and Dial (left) was originally called the Plough, but around 1908 the pub was extended to take in the building next door and became the Plough and Dial. It closed for business in 1966. A fine picture taken around 1905 shows that the added part had been a butcher's shop (and a public house called the Dial) run by the Crawley family.

SANDERS
CENTRAL
WIRELESS STORES
STOP

Hitchin, Bancroft c1955 H89035
Bancroft was said to be one of the most beautiful streets in England by the artist F L Griggs in the 1890s, and it still shows a certain charm. The building in the distance stands at Moss's Corner. The firm of W Moss became the largest group of shops in the district - at one time they had 10 outlets. We can see one of their shops on the opposite side of the road close to the unfortunate concrete lamp standard.

S O N
Sara Lewis

Hitchin, Churchyard c1965 H89065
At this date, Churchyard was a centre for bustling trade and commerce. Even nearly 50 years ago, the area was pedestrianised, giving shoppers safe access to Finlays the confectioners and tobacconists and Baxters the butchers. Such shops would not have been out of place when the first Frith photographs of Hitchin were taken. The post (centre left) marks the site of a set of iron gates which prevented vehicles from entering the yard during church services. The Churchyard was used as a location for the pre-war film 'Dandy Dick' starring the late Will Hay. Thirty years before this photograph, workmen altering Day's fruit shop at Nos 12 and 13 Churchyard broke into a secret room where they found a skeleton, a vat of wine and a chalice. The wine was drunk, the chalice donated to the local museum and the skeleton ... it is not recorded what happened to the skeleton!

Hitchin
The River Hiz 1931 84198
Only the clothes worn by the children give a clue to the date of this photograph. The vista has hardly changed in 60 years. However, in the period up to around 1900, the River Hiz was an open sewer used for household and personal effluent, and this area was the site of slums and cheek-by-jowl dwellings. Further down, towards Bancroft and Nightingale Road, the tannery and other industrial works poured their waste into the river. Only the lavender works may have offset the obnoxious smell of the Hiz!

Letchworth, St Mary's Church 1922 71909

The name of the town of Letchworth appears to derive from 'lecha weorthig', 'the farm by the rivulet'. There is no mention of a church here at the time of Domesday, although there was woodland for 100 pigs. Robert Gernon held the manor, and his name is remembered in Gernon Road, home of the District Council Offices. St Mary's lies just off Letchworth Lane, some distance from the original town, but close to Letchworth Manor.

Letchworth, St Mary's Church 1924 75603

The tiny flint-walled church of St Mary was rebuilt c1135, and is one of the smallest in the county. It is only 60ft long, and consists of a nave and a lower chancel. There is no tower, just a small bell turret which was added around 1500. A single bell of about 1370 survives, and is tolled regularly. The neatly tended graveyard stands as a testament to the many generations of Letchworth people who have worshipped here.

Letchworth
Letchworth Hall Hotel 1922 71910
King Edward I transferred the manor of Letchworth to the Knights Templar. When the order was dissolved in 1312, it passed to the Knights Hospitallers and eventually to the Lytton family of Knebworth. Some of the fabric of Letchworth Hall dates from the late 1400s, but most is the result of subsequent restorations, particularly that of the early 1700s. In 1796, Letchworth Hall was bought by John Williamson, a baker from Baldock. It was eventually purchased by the Garden City Pioneer Company in 1903, and opened as a hotel in 1904. A licence to sell alcohol was granted in 1935, enraging many of the Garden City's teetotal inhabitants.

Letchworth, St Paul's Church 1924 75604
It is difficult to realise that the apparently remote St Paul's church now stands adjacent to a busy roundabout at the junction of Pixmore Way and Baldock Road. Construction was started in 1919 on this Gothic-style 'Victory' church designed by Arthur Heron Ryan-Tenison; the photograph shows St Paul's shortly after its consecration early in 1924. It is now an Evangelical church.

Letchworth, Leys Avenue c1950 L39002
We are looking westwards along Leys Avenue; we can just see the last of the Georgian-style shops and flats in the distance. The more modern Burtons tailors breaks the line and starts the row of more traditional buildings with their fine pargetted gables. In front of the Morris 8 is parked what must be one of the last of Letchworth traders' hand carts.

Letchworth
Leys Avenue c1960
L39082
Originally built for Barclays, the Midland Bank was built in 1908 in the Georgian style from a design by Hugh Seebohm. It was intended to mirror a building on the opposite corner, but the project was never pursued. The Georgian style can be seen following along the left side of Leys Avenue and on Station Road at Lloyd's Bank (left).

IRENE
Say it with Flowers

Letchworth, Leys Avenue c1960 L39034
Named after the field on which it was built, Leys Avenue was, even in 1960, a busy shopping thoroughfare. The pace of life was only slightly slower than today, although standards of traffic safety might be questioned. The Commer van, 'Say it with Flowers' (left), is rather close to the zebra crossing and has been parked there for some time - it appears in the same position in the photograph of Barclay's Bank!

NORTON RADIO
A.M. & E.G. TAYLOR

Letchworth
The Spirella Factory c1950
L39007
This building was often known as 'Castle Corset'. The Spirella Company came to Letchworth in 1910. The new factory was commissioned in 1912, and was built over the following eight years. In his book 'Letchworth, the First Garden City', Mervyn Miller says, 'Spirella not only dominated visually, but equally provided a natural focus for the town's social life during the inter-war period'. There were few people living in Letchworth at that time who did not have connection with (or wore a product of) the Spirella factory.

Norton, The Village c1950 N196038
The village of Norton dates from the Saxon period. One of the earliest references to Norton is a grant by Offa of Mercia to the monastery at St Albans. A priest is mentioned in Domesday, and it is possible that his wooden church stood on the site of the present church of St Nicholas, which was dedicated in 1119. In the church is a memorial to a little girl named Cole who was born in September 1752 and died in February 1752 - of course, between these dates, the calendar was reformed! Tea rooms and public houses, like the Three Horse Shoes (left), have always been a necessity in the village - when the estate was being investigated for purchase by the First Garden City company, Norton End's drinking water was found to contain 14% sewage.

Norton, Post Office Corner c1950
N196001
Now part of a strictly controlled conservation area, this group of shops on the corner of Green Lane and Norton Road blend into the environment. The Standard 8 and the pre-war Morris 8 complement the view, and the youngster on the tricycle reminds us that Norton was still a tranquil backwater. Only the concrete 1930s telephone kiosk seems out of place.

Baldock, Hitchin Street c1955 B9011
Hitchin Street formed part of the complex of parallel trackways which made up the Icknield Way. Baldock provided a resting place for travellers, and little has changed in the 1000 or so years of its life. Even in the mid 1920s, almost every other building is an inn or a tavern - only the concrete lamp post and the television aerials identify this as the 20th century.

Baldock, St Mary's Church 1925 77103
The tower of Baldock church was built in the 14th century. It supports an octagonal lantern surmounted by a traditional Hertfordshire spike, which can be seen for miles around. Tradition says that three Knights Templar are buried in the stone coffins in the church wall. In the churchyard stands a gravestone to Henry George Brown who died aged 10 years and 10 months on 20 April 1861: 'How soon I was cut down, when innocent at play. The wind it blew a scaffold down and took my life away.'

Baldock, The George and Dragon Hotel c1955 B9003

In the 1920s and 1930s, the George and Dragon Hotel was a popular stopping-place for cyclists and walkers following the route of the Icknield Way. For the more discerning 'Commercials and Motorists' it provided 'wines, spirits and billiards'. The George and Dragon stands opposite the corner of Sun Street and adjacent to the site of the Sun public house (later the Victoria.) Only the 1950s 'Keep Left' sign differs from the view today.

PP 3143

Baldock, White Horse Street 1925 77097
The Icknield Way was a pre-Roman, Iron Age trading route running along the northern border of Hertfordshire. At Baldock it formed the length of White Horse Street and Hitchin Street. Inns and beer houses served the needs of travellers and waggon drivers - the Chequers stands on the left and the George and Dragon faces us in the distance. The photographer stood with his back to the site of the White Horse, which burnt down in the 1860s. Fred Butler, who ran the petrol station on the left, started business in the 1890s as a bicycle retailer. Past Butlers on the left is the Rose and Crown, which provided overnight garaging for motorists and was strongly endorsed by both the AA and the RAC. A far cry from the days when the four-legged horse power ruled and Baldock's annual horse fair took place in White Horse Street.

Wilson
CAPSTAN
CIGARETTES

Baldock, White Horse Street c1955 B9016
The centre of Baldock, at the junction of the market place and the Icknield Way, is dominated by the imposing Town Hall and Old Fire Station, opened on 25 November 1897 to commemorate Queen Victoria's jubilee. The Town Hall now houses Baldock's fascinating museum. The lonely Vauxhall E Series (centre) drives towards Letchworth along Hitchin Street past the shops and inns. Today the traffic is a solid, almost immovable mass, and few cyclists risk their lives shopping at Wilsons, the tobacconists (left), or at Pattersons (centre right), who were once saddlers and leather workers. This is a marked contrast to a now busy town soon to be subdued by the construction of a by-pass.

Baldock High Street 1925
77096
The market town of Baldock developed at the junction of a Roman road and the ancient Icknield Way in the mid 1100s. It is said that the Knights Templar named the town 'Baudacum' - a Latinised from of Baghdad - and that this evolved into Baldock. The market still meets on the original site each week, but on a non-market day in the 1920s, Baldock has an air of almost desertion. On the right, in the background, is Quenby's garage with its 'swing-arm' petrol pump. On the opposite side of the road, almost obscured by the dark shadow of the Town Hall, stands a Great War gun carriage.

Ashwell, West End c1955
A149001
Little has changed at this junction on the roads to Newnham and Hinxworth, known as West End and Back Street. The first token reference to the growing traffic can be identified in the reflective pillar mounted on the boundary wall (centre). The cottages were owned by Joshua Page, one of the many local brewers, as accommodation for his workers. Later it was the site of a fish and chip shop run by Fred Harris.

Ashwell, High Street c1955 A149006
This was clearly a successful village which had made its fortune by the weaving and cloth trade, as well as through agriculture. Later, in the mid 1800s, coprolite extraction brought prosperity to the landowners and inhabitants: phosphotic nodules, mined locally, were washed with dilute sulphuric acid, ground to a powder and sold as a powerful fertilizer. One of the gang-masters of the mining teams was a certain Mr Fison. The Foresters Cottages, in the right foreground, were to be demolished in a few years after the photograph was taken, but were saved and extensively restored in the 1960s through the Hertfordshire Building Preservation Trust and Hertfordshire County Council.

Ashwell, The Museum c1955 A149009
This early 16th-century timber-framed house, formerly owned by St John's College, Cambridge and earlier by Westminster Abbey, was used by the village as the Town House for the collection of rents and tithes. In the late 1920s it was in a dilapidated state and about to be demolished, but it was purchased for £25 to house the bygones and objects of local interest collected by Albert Sheldrick and John Bray. As Ashwell Museum, it was opened to the public on 29 November 1930. Over 70 years later, it continues to thrive as one of the best small museums in Hertfordshire.

Ashwell
High Street c1955 A149017
St Mary's church, most of which was built in the 14th century, demonstrates the wealth of the village. It also recalls the tragedy wreaked on the countryside by the Black Death and plague in the form of a graffito, '1350, wretched, fierce, violent - the dregs of the people survive to tell the tale'. It is difficult to imagine a devastated village when we look back at this tranquil High Street. Tommy Dennis's butcher's shop (centre right) was renowned for its ornate topiary and for the life-like bull's head mounted on the board across the building. The red, green and gold sign has been an important and attractive feature of the High Street for over 100 years.

Royston
Therfield Heath 1929 81899

Skirted by the Icknield Way on the right, the expanse of Therfield Heath originally stretched from the boundary of Baldock to Royston. Traditionally an area of recreation (King James I exercised his Royston-kennelled hunting hounds here), this peaceful view of the Heath was photographed before the installation of football and cricket pitches. In the 1800s, the Royston Militia camped and performed manoeuvres on the Heath, whilst archaeologists, fascinated by the tumuli, carried out extensive excavations. The memorial was erected in 1900 (says Alfred Kingston in his 1906 'History of Royston') in remembrance of Queen Victoria. Later, during the Second World War, a camp for Italian prisoners of war was built on the Heath.

Royston
The Stone c1955 R63011
It is said that the town took its name from Lady Roysia's Stone, and that the stone itself was the base for the Market Cross. Royston is a relatively modern town - it is not mentioned in the Domesday Book - which grew up at the crossing of Ermine Street and the Icknield Way; it was not officially recognised until the late 1800s. The town was 'carved' out of four parishes - Bassingbourn and Melbourn in Cambridgeshire and Therfield and Barkway in Hertfordshire. Lady Roysia's manor of Newsells lay in the parish of Barkway. The stone has been moved several times, and is now located on the opposite side of the Icknield Way.

SOLD BY
JANUARY

**Royston
High Street c1965**
R63038
It is difficult to realise that this was once the main Roman road from London to Godmanchester and on to York. The photograph was taken shortly after the High Street was closed to through traffic; the untidy houses on the left will soon become desirable town residences and shops. The Bull (right), once the scene of disreputable activities, was by this time a respectable hotel offering accommodation and facilities for banquets, as well as snacks and lunches.

Barley, The Fox and Hounds c1955 B405022
One of two Hertfordshire inns with cross-street signs (the other is the Four Swans at Waltham Cross), the Fox and Hounds moved to its present site in 1955 after a disastrous fire at the old building in the High Street in August 1950. The present pub was previously known as the Waggon and Horses. In the distance, under the sign, stands the church of St Margaret of Antioch. The unusual lantern and spire were erected in 1872 to a design by Butterfield.

Royston, Priory Gardens c1955
R63034
With not an ancient building in sight, we would be forgiven for believing that this is the centre of one of Hertfordshire's 20th-century garden cities. Nothing could be further from the truth. Just out of sight to the left stands the ancient parish church of Royston, whilst behind the photographer is the original priory from which the gardens take their name. This quiet spot in the centre of this bustling market town is now covered with tennis courts, a children's playground and extensive rose gardens.

Royston, Barkway Road 1929 81893
The descent from Barkway, the second highest point in Hertfordshire, down to Royston, one of the lowest places in the county, was a nightmare for horse-drawn traffic and cyclists. Fortunately the chalk from the quarry, hidden behind the hedge on the right, provided material for a solid surface. Although the area is now substantially built up, the group of dwellings on the left still survive intact.

Barkway, High Street c1965
B281015
The school (left) was built in 1840, and provided education for the children of Barkway and Reed. This fine building is remarkably original, and stands on the site of the old Market Square. The white building (right) was the village butcher's shop - joints of meat were hung from the trees; beyond it is the three-gabled Town House. It is said that the ornate staircase in the Town House came from Standon Lordship. The white shed on the left stands next to the village pond where the villagers skated in winter.

◄ **Anstey, Puttocks End c1955** A156007

These thatched cottages are on either side of the road to Brent Pelham at the eastern, outer reaches of Anstey. Puttock's End, one of the highest points in Hertfordshire, was the home of the Glasscock, Flack and Catley families, whose local pedigrees go back to the 1500s. The village boasted a good, pure supply of spring water, and the pump was used by all of the local communities.

◄ **Barkway, High Street c1965** B281019

Barkway spanned the main route from London to Cambridge, and it was only the coming of the railways in the 1850s that transformed it into a countryside backwater. The building on the right with the tall brick chimneys is the Reading Room, erected in the 1860s to provide a respectable meeting place for the young men of the village. On the left, the Chaise and Pair, one of five inns still functioning in the village in 1965, offered fine beer and accommodation. It closed for business in 1993.

▼ **Wyddial, The Village 1923** 74927

Sad to say, the fine thatched house and barn have not survived; only the row of Rose Cottages stand today as a reminder of the tiny village of Wyddial. The community grew up on the road between Buntingford (or Layston, as it was then called) and the villages of Barkway and Anstey. Wyddial Hall, in 1923 the home of the Heaton-Ellis family, stands on the high ground about 1/4 mile to the right of the photographer, and can be seen for miles around. Wyddial's greatest claim to fame is that is cut in half by the Meridian Line - a tiny cast iron commemoration post has been set up opposite the entrance to Wyddial Hall.

◄ **Buntingford, Chipping Village c1955** B245037

Spanning the old Ermine Street (now the A10 road), Chipping was an early, but unsuccessful, attempt at developing a market town. The Royal Oak (right) burnt down in the 1970s, and all signs of it have now disappeared - only the small housing development called Royal Oak Close reminds us that it ever existed. On the opposite side of the road the telephone kiosk stands in front of the houses which form The Square.

Buntingford
Royston Road 1923 74925
The building on the right, now demolished, stood on the corner of what is now Vicarage Road, and was the first county library in the town. Mrs Crouch and her daughter are at the door of their cottage. This, too, has gone, and Freman Drive cuts now across the site. Of all the buildings, only the house in the distance on the left, No 1 Ermine Street, survives. It reminds us that Buntingford High Street and Royston Road follow the line of the Roman Ermine Street.

Buntingford, High Street c1955 B245007
We are looking south. The shop in the right foreground is now Mark Doel's butcher's shop; the modern library is a few doors further down towards the Angel, whose sign can be seen in the distance. Today, the suspended street lighting has disappeared, and although Buntingford has a major by-pass, traffic is heavier than the two cyclists and the solitary parked delivery van.

Buntingford, High Street c1955 B245033
The street follows the course of the Roman road Ermine Street, and is typically without any sign of a bend. On the left, the white timber-framed, jettied building was the Bell Inn, which closed around 1880; it is now a gift shop. It is said that Queen Elizabeth I stayed at the Bell on a journey north. Contemporary with her visit are a number of unique wall paintings. Behind the Bell were extensive barns for stabling and accommodation for blacksmiths and grooms.

Sketchley
CLEANERS
WOMAN'S
REALM
Today

Buntingford High Street c1965

B245066

The turret above the passageway adjacent to the newsagent contains the town's one-handed clock. One of the earliest records of the Town Clock was in 1618, when local townspeople were asked to contribute to its enhancement. In 1558, Henry Skynner bequeathed the building to the poor of Buntingford. The brick-faced building with arched windows was the Angel Inn, which had an orchard and yard where the customers played quoits. Great Lane or Church Lane, on the right, leads down to the River Rib and to Wyddial.

Buntingford
Market Hill c1955 B245015

The public pump (left) stands in front of the Crown pub - it was built in 1690 and extensively restored in 1993. The cover was built by F J Robinson to celebrate Queen Victoria's Diamond Jubilee. The market was originally chartered in 1542 and resurrected in 1920; a weekly auction was held under the trees, and the cattle and sheep were held here in pens. The tall house on the right was the Manse - it became a shop in the 1930s. The white building behind the RAC sign (right) was at one time the Master Tanner's House.

Buntingford
The River Rib 1922 71887
The bridge over the Rib, built in 1852, leads to the Causeway and Layston church. The Cottage, on the corner, faces onto River Green and looks towards the right of the photograph and Pig's Nose, originally a c1500 farm shed but now a residence. The reasons for it name are lost in obscurity, although it has been suggested that the shape of the plot is reminiscent of a pig's snout!

Buntingford
The Causeway 1923
74924
The Causeway leads from the town of Buntingford to the original, and now derelict, parish church of St Bartholomew, Layston. The trees on the left fell victim to Dutch elm disease, and have now been replaced. On the right is the garden wall to Little Court, and behind the trees stands Layston School, skirted on the west by Paddock Road. The open land to the left of the trees is now the playing fields of Layston School.

Westmill, The Village Green c1955 W295002

If, as has been reported, it is not the most beautiful village in Hertfordshire, Westmill is certainly among the most photographed. The pump and its unique cover dominates the Green, with the cottages known as Pilgrim's Row behind. They are named after Samuel Pilgrim, who built them early in the early 1700s. The house on the right of the row, covered with ivy, is Parliament House. St Mary's church has some Saxon features, but much was lost during the Victorian rebuilding. The tower was restored in 2001. On the left is the village post office and tearooms, and to its right stands the fine turreted village hall.

Braughing, Hay Street c1955 B411027e

On the B1368 road a mile or so north of Braughing stands the small community of Hay Street. This tranquil group of cottages lies alongside what was the main road from London to Huntingdon, and probably takes its name from a corruption of 'High Street'. Today the traffic speeds past the cottages, and on occasions the boarded building in the foreground takes direct hits from heavy lorries. It has been rebuilt many times over the years, but still retains its original character. The house in the distance was once the village shop.

Braughing
The Post Office Stores c1955 B411027c

Little has changed since this photograph was taken. The garage on the left has been replaced by two houses, but almost fifty years later, the post office still sports its black exposed timber on white rendering. Braughing is a favourite stopping-place for classic car runs, and the Morris 8 and Austin 10 would not appear out of place today on summer week-end afternoons. The enamel-faced letter box still survives, but it has now been blocked up, sad to say; today letters have to be posted in something more modern. The post office was once the Bell pub, and the sign, a solid wooden bell, is still in place under the porch.

◀ **Standon, The Paper Mill c1965** S377006
Previously a corn mill, the building was converted to manufacture hand-made paper in 1713. More than forty people were employed here collecting rags, which were sorted by women and children, washed in the river and laid out to dry in Laundry Meadow opposite the mill to the right of the photograph. The rags were then cut up and pounded to form the fibres in the paper. In 1865, the mill was converted to a saw mill and later to an engineering workshop. It is now a private residence. The ford does not cut straight across the Rib, but runs along the river bed and then emerges further down stream on the opposite bank. Motorists use the ford at their peril: it is susceptible to flash flooding, and many an unwary traveller has found himself and his car floating away down stream.

◀ **Standon, High Street c1965** S377004

The large piece of puddingstone (we get a good view of it in S377013) is reputed to have been turned up by a plough on a field called 'Plain', and it was set up in the street opposite the church gate. It was later moved to the triangle in front of Groom's shop in 1904. The Top Shop has gone, but the stone remains. Hertfordshire puddingstone is a naturally forming conglomerate of well-rounded gravel in a cement-like matrix. Often confused with concrete, it is relatively common in the eastern and central part of Hertfordshire, but not unknown in other glacial areas. The road on the left leads down to Paper Mill and the ford across the River Rib.

▼ **Standon, High Street and the Church c1965** S377011

St Mary's church dominates the High Street skyline. Unique in Hertfordshire, Standon parish church has a detached bell tower and a porch at the west end rather than on the south wall. It is built on the side of a hill, and a flight of steps leads up from the nave to the altar. Although the building dates from the 14th century, the foundations are Saxon. The houses past Burr Meadow and the Windmill pub (left) are known locally as the Three Bears - Little Bear, Middle Bear (Ivy Cottage) and Big Bear (Standon House). On the first Monday in May the Standon Morris Men host groups from all over the region, and a grand assembly of morris men dance on the High Street.

◀ **Standon, The Stone and the School c1965** S377013

Education here probably started in 1135, when the Knights Hospitallers built their hospice on the site. Some of the material used in its construction dates from Roman times. The school was renamed Roger de Clare School in 1969 when Mr Pritchard was head teacher; it moved to new premises in 1974, when the building was converted to housing. As well as dancing on May Day holiday, the Standon Morris Men gather at the Stone at sunrise to dance a welcome to the first day of May.

Much Hadham St Andrew's Church 1899 44879
Little has changed in the 100 years since this photograph was taken. On the left, peeping through the trees, are the white gables of the Old Rectory; in the foreground are the meadows skirting the River Ash which were part of the grounds of the Bishop of London's palace, just out of view to the right. The view is from the east, and shows the fine tracery of the church window and the traditional Hertfordshire spike on the tower.

Much Hadham, St Andrew's Church 1899 44881
Some of the windows in St Andrew's have been replaced by others designed by the sculptor and artist Henry Moore, who lived at nearby Hoglands in Perry Green. The Anglican church welcomed the congregation of Holy Cross Roman Catholic church in 1982, and they have continued to use the church jointly. St Andrew's was built in the 13th century, and the tower was added late in the 1500s by Bishop Braybrook.

Bishop's Stortford, General View 1899 44282
The spire of St Michael's church dominates the skyline. When the tower was found to be unstable, it was strengthened and the spire raised to 182 feet. The roofs of four maltings mark the towpath of the River Stort. Some of these maltings have now been converted into dwellings.

Bishop's Stortford, The Maltings on the River Stort 1903 49765
By 1940, only 6 out of the 17 maltings in the town were in operation. Barley and fuel for the furnaces were brought to Stortford by water, and latterly by rail. Processing of the barley into malt took place from September to June; during this time the furnaces were never extinguished, and a sweet-smelling pall covered the town. The sacks of malt and barley husks, for cattle feed, were loaded onto barges and transported to London.

Bishop's Stortford Bridge Street 1922

71842

A ballad of 1843 refers to the building on the left as 'the Ugly Black Lion'. In the late 1890s, the Black Lion public house was extensively altered and restored by Mr Glasscock; by removing the plaster and exposing the windows, he attempted to return the building to its original 1600s style. On the opposite side of Bridge Street stands the Star Tavern, which was first recorded in 1616. A nice 1920 Ford Model T stands outside the tobacconist (left), and the lady in the foreground prepares to rest her bicycle against a cast iron gas lamp standard.

STORES
OFFICE OF THE
HERTS AND ESSEX
OBSERVER

Bishop's Stortford North Street 1909

61338

This view looks southwards towards the Corn Exchange, with the Chantry behind the photographer. On the left are the offices of the Herts and Essex Observer, where Harry Murdon printed the newspaper for 73 years until 1961. On the right are the arches of the council offices. In 1905, the fire brigade erected an arch across North Street to welcome King Edward VII on his visit to the town. The ornate water pump supplies a trough for weary horses.

Bishop's Stortford Castle Gardens 1922

71847

Castle Gardens were laid out in 1905 on part of the old town. The cenotaph, engraved with the names of the 200 who died in the Great War, was unveiled on 3 April 1921, and the first memorial service took place there on 11 November 1922. The photograph was taken from the Mound, the site of the original Waytemore Castle, which was given by William the Conqueror to Maurice, Bishop of London.

Bishop's Stortford Chantry Gate 1899 44293
The 16th-century Chantry in Hadham Road was built on the site of the original priest's house on lands granted under the will of Baldwyn Victor. Just out of sight, under the gate, are the so-called 'ruins'. These, along with the arch, were moved from either St Michael's or one of the London churches and rebuilt at the Chantry by Sir Walter Gilbey.

Bishop's Stortford Castle Gardens and War Memorial 1922 71849
A Peace Parade was held at Stortford in July 1919 when the plans for the memorial in Castle Gardens were announced. By-laws forbade the beating of carpets and driving of cattle through the gardens. The glass-houses on the right produced flowers for town events. The practice was discontinued in the 1960s, when Mr Forth the head gardener retired.

Bishop's Stortford Potter Street c1950 B104010
Behind the Morris 8, Church Street turns to the left with Boots 'Cash Chemist' on the corner. Today Potter Street is one-way - the traffic in the photograph is facing in the wrong direction. The fascias to Boots and beyond hide a range of early timber-framed buildings. Disons, on the right at 25 Potter Street, replaced William Rowlandson's draper's shop which occupied the site in the 1920s. The town's great claim to fame is that it is the birthplace of Cecil Rhodes, founder of Rhodesia.

Bishop's Stortford, Hockerill Street c1955 B104031

Hockerill Street leads downhill into the town from the crossroads with the London to Newmarket road. Each corner was once occupied by a public house or inn. In 1896, at the centre of the crossroads, an ornate stone fountain was erected to the memory of Mr George Brampston Houblon-Archer (alias Brigadier Eyre) of Great Hallingbury as a gift from Ezra and Eliza Eyre. When it became a hazard to traffic, it was moved to Castle Gardens. In 1913, the shop on the right sold R White's lemonade, which was manufactured in Walkern.

Bishop's Stortford, The Boar's Head, High Street c1955 B104018

The earliest record of the Boar's Head is in 1630. The beam over the fireplace is reputed to have supported the figures of Christ, St Mary and St John across the rood screen in St Michael's church. This was removed from the church in 1547, but soon put back in place. However, in 1570 it was removed again, and found a permanent home in the Boar's Head. A tunnel, whose entrance can still be seen in the cellar, is said to connect to Waytemore Castle. But beware! The cellar is also said to be haunted by the ghost of a Grey Lady.

Thorley, The Church of St James the Great 1899 44877

Some visitors to Hertfordshire think that Thorley lies on the main road between Bishop's Stortford and Sawbridgeworth - this should, correctly, be called Thorley Street. Frith has photographed the church at the true village of Thorley about a mile to the west of the town. In 1899 it was a declining community, with a few cottages and this isolated church. The recent boom in housing development has seen the expansion of Bishop's Stortford up to the edge of Thorley but the church, parts of which date from the 12th century, and the cottages survive at the southern end of Church Lane, close to the pond. Francis Burloes, who was given the living of Thorley in 1594 by Queen Elizabeth I, was one of the translators of the Authorised Version of the Bible.

Sawbridgeworth, London Road 1903 51096

We are looking southwards from Walnut Tree Corner, and London Road is deserted apart from the wagon standing outside the Gate public house (centre left). The Gate was originally one of a pair of cottages built by Samuel Legerton in 1830; the northernmost of the cottages was converted to the public house around 1843. All the wooden fences still stand today, although many of the cast iron railings have disappeared, probably as part of scrap metal collection during the two world wars. The building between the lamp post and the telegraph pole on the left was until recently a builders' hire shop, but is now Unwins off-licence.

Sawbridgeworth London Road 1903

51098

Towards the southern end of London Road, the 'tip-up' cart is parked waiting for its horse to be harnessed, whilst a milk cart (left) winds slowly up the hill towards the Congregational church close to the junction with Maylins Drive. Sawbridgeworth was renowned for the longevity of its inhabitants. In 1869, John Edwin Cussans, the respected Hertfordshire historian, noted that Mrs Elizabeth Puckle, who was born here in 1765, was still alive at nearby High Wych. The house on the right, Boatmans, still stands today.

◄ **Sawbridgeworth Hyde Hall 1903** 51103

Hyde Hall was probably given to Geoffrey de Mandeville after the Norman Conquest. It passed down through the Jocelyn family, whose monuments can be seen in the church of St Mary the Great. Hyde Hall was extended in 1806 and completely refurbished in 1869. When part of the property was sold in 1983 for £80,000, Hyde Hall was described as 'a magnificent mansion enjoying 40 acres of maintained ground'.

Sawbridgeworth The Church of St Mary the Great 1903 51100

St Mary's contains a particularly fine group of sculptures, and is renowned for its collection of monumental brasses. The church was built in the late 14th century, and was extensively restored in 1868. In the old days the interior of this church was strewn with pea straw, but one year it caught fire and the interior was considerably damaged. The tradition was immediately terminated!

Sawbridgeworth, Vantorts Road c1960 S67030

The King William IV public house, dating from 1862, is the first in a row of noteworthy buildings in Vantorts Road. At one time it had a small brewery attached which served beer through a surviving range of unique pumps. Next door stands the Masonic Hall, and Fair Green House is in the distance.

Sawbridgeworth Bell Street c1960 S67032

Bell Street, part of the original town of Sawbridgeworth, runs from London road eastwards towards the church and the school. The site of the annual horse fair up to the early 1900s, it is named after the Bell public house, which stood opposite the sack hoist at the maltings. The proposed removal of the tree by the maltings in the 1980s was the subject of a general protest. Laundresses would have hung their washing to dry on the field, now a cricket pitch, behind the buildings on the right. In the 1960s, Achille Serre provided a dry cleaning service to the inhabitants.

Hunsdon, The Green c1965 H475006
The war memorial stands south of the Crown Inn, at the junction of the High Street and Acorn Street. Acorn Street, now redirected so that the memorial is next to the Crown's car park, leads to Hunsdon House. The original Hunsdon House (the present building is relatively modern) was built by Sir John Oldfield (or Oldhall) around 1447; it is said that after the divorce of Henry VIII and Ann Boleyn, their children were virtually imprisoned here.

Hunsdon, High Street c1965 H475008
We can just see the second Hunsdon public house, the Fox and Hounds, in the distance on the left, with houses in Tanner's Way (on the opposite side of the road) behind. The Fox and Hounds was a popular meeting-place for London cyclists in the traffic-free 1920s. Hunsdon is one of the tidiest and most attractive villages in Hertfordshire, and proudly displays the Best Kept Village trophy. The black and white timbered building on the right is the Village Hall. The jetty of the adjacent house is supported by a pair of ornate mythical creatures.

Hunsdon, St Dunstan's Church c1965 H475009
The architectural style suggests that St Dunstan's was built towards the end of the 15th century, although there is a record of a church on the site as early as 1291. It was heavily renovated in 1851 during the ministry of the Rev Richard W Thackery (rector from 1845 to 1861.) The church had been covered in a thick growth of ivy, but by the time of this photograph, it had been cut back to reveal the true beauty of the structure. The main entrance to the church, unusually for Hertfordshire, is via the north porch - traditionally the south porch was used..

Wareside, Babbs Green c1955 W290003
These houses, built in 1933, are called Coanwood Cottages. They face onto the road leading to Wareside village centre. The van (right) is driving down Fanhams' Hall Lane from Ware, and may be about to turn left past Appleton Farm and Baker's End. The ditch on the right drains across the road into the delightfully named Nimney Bourne near Holy Trinity church just behind the photographer.

◀ **Stanstead Abbots, All Nations Missionary College c1960**
S181017
Easneye, originally called Isneye, was the home of the Buxton family after 1866, when Thomas Fowell Buxton purchased the estate - it comprised thick woodland. The new house, completed in 1869, was designed by Alfred Waterhouse, who was also the architect of St Pancras station and the Natural History Museum. The exterior of the house was used as St Trinian's School in the series of films starring Alistair Sim and George Cole. Today, Easneye is home to the All Nations College for Missionaries.

Wareside, The Village c1955 W290006
Wareside is known by locals as the Treacle Mines! Philpot's General Stores was also used as a slaughterhouse until the early 1950s, when it became the post office. It closed in 1990, and for a short while was an antiques shop which only opened on Friday afternoons. The property is now a private residence. It is said that in 1834, the building was used as an elementary school under the will of Humphrey Spencer; in his will of 1633, he left £100 to educate four poor children in reading and writing. On the opposite side of the road is the Chequers public house. It dates from the 16th century, and was originally the Chequers and Punch Bowl. At the end of the 19th century, Wareside boasted seven public houses.

Stanstead Abbots The Village 1929 81859c
The five-gabled Red Lion Inn, which provided accommodation and garaging for motorists, carries the date 1538 on the centre gable. In the distance, the Old Clock House was originally a school founded in 1635 by Sir Edward Baesh; by 1929 it had become a restaurant and tea rooms. The road to the left, Capel Lane (sometimes called Church Lane, and later Park Lane), leads to All Nations College at Easneye, whilst the road on the right leads to Cat's Hill and Roydon in Essex.

Stanstead Abbots, The View from Cats Hill c1960 S181005
Running downhill into Stanstead Abbots from the north-east, Cats Hill presents a formidable hazard to modern motorists. It was not so in the 1960s, without a vehicle in view. In the 1600s it would not have been the horse-drawn wagons that the visitor first noticed, but more likely the smell, for Stanstead Abbots was a centre for the manufacture of woad. Queen Elizabeth would not have a woad mill within five miles of any of her palaces, and it is reported that at Stanstead visitors were 'constrained to stop their nosses as they go bye, the stink is so grate'. Today, Cats Hill is notorious for out-of-control vehicles careering into the dwellings.

IRONMONGERS
BLACKWELLS
ROOFINGS
TIMBER
RANGE

Stanstead Abbots High Street 1929
81861

The fine saloon car in the foreground, probably a year-old Morris 20, bearing the registration number YU6523, appears in many contemporary photographs of Stanstead Abbots - does it still survive today? On the right is John William Hodgin's draper's shop, which was earlier the post office and run by A Blackby. Further down was William W Ray, a confectioner and tobacconist; he offered afternoon teas, and was an agent for Daren Bread. Next was Frank Andrews, a saddler, who supplemented his income by repairing cycles. On the left was Mrs Mabel Harwood, a milliner, whose business was in competition with the Misses M & H Bishop, then J Catesby, the 'cheapest ironmonger in town.' Just visible is the Three Fishes, which also served as the post office.

Stanstead Abbots
The River Lee Navigation
1929 81866

The flood plain of the Lea was broad and provided rich, fertile soil for agriculture. Further south, the market gardens and nurseries of Hoddesdon and Cheshunt provided employment for thousands of local people, and the greenhouses covered acres of land. In earlier times, it is said, the Danes sailed up the river past Ware just east of Hertford, where they established a short-lived settlement in the marshy valley.

Stanstead Abbots, The River Lee Navigation 1929 81865

The network of canals developed mainly in the 18th century before the arrival of the railway. The complex of rivers and canals at Stanstead St Margarets and Stanstead Abbots bring together the Lea, the New River, Stanstead Mill Stream and, slightly further to the south, the River Stort. It has been a source of confusion to visitors that the river is called the Lea, whilst the Navigation is called the Lee! No one seems to know the reason for the difference.

Ware The Forage Stores 1925 77109c

John Page & Sons, the owners of the Forage Stores, at 96 High Street, supplied a wide range of pet food - Armitage Chicken Food, Spratts Ovals and Chikko for Chicks. His great business rival was William Page of 31 High Street, who sold exactly the same products. Next door is E W Nicholls; then comes Taylors the tobacconist's, which in the 1890s was a two-storey building occupied by Campbell the grocer. One of the hotel taxis which regularly operated from the railway station waits for its customer outside the shops.

Ware, The Allen & Hanbury Works c1965 W24069

The Domesday survey covering Ware mentions two mills. It is possible that one of them lay on the site of Ware Mill, later part of the factory of Allen & Hanbury. The company was founded in 1715, and in 1898 they bought the old mill to construct their Ware factory. An important part of their production was special dietary products for invalids and children, including Allenburys Malted Rusks; the packaging showed views of the River Lea at Ware. The company was taken over by the Glaxo Group in 1958, but continued as Allen Hanbury until 1978.

IRONMONGERS
THE WARE HARDWARE STORES

Ware
High Street 1925
77110

Shortly after this photograph was taken, the Ware Hardware Stores closed, and the building became tearooms catering for visitors to the town. In the 1970s, it housed H Donaghue, the fish, game and poultry merchants. On the left, along West Street, stood the Crown and Anchor public house next door to the shop selling 'home-made pork pies and sandwiches'. The grocery shop on the right had been owned by Samuel and later Ebenezer Giffin. At the time of the photograph it was owned by William Cullen, and passed in the 1940s to Swan & Nickolds. The furthest building on the right side of the road is the Saracen's Head, which was demolished in October 1957.

Ware, Amwell End 1925 77112
Ware is packed full of interesting buildings and streets, but nothing it has to offer surpasses Amwell End. This seemingly quiet street has a bustle of yards and courts behind the facades of the shops and dwellings. Amwell End was the original toll road entry to Ware from the south until the building of the bridge. At the far end, it is crossed by the railway and the river. Flooding was a major problem, and many of the buildings were regularly under water. At the far end on the right we can see the canopied Astoria Cinema. Even the visit of Cliff Richard and his original backing group, the Drifters, in the 1960s could not save the Astoria, and it became one of the first victims of the surge towards bingo. The buildings facing the policeman have been demolished and replaced by a range of modern shops. To the left of them is the entrance to Chapel Yard.

Ware, The High Street 1925 77111
We are looking westwards; the building on the right was originally the Town Hall. Built on the Market Place, it was erected by public subscription in 1827 as an arcaded corn exchange with meeting rooms above. The enterprise failed, and the building was soon sold as shops. Stallabrass the butcher was an early tenant, and in the 1920s it was taken by Home and Colonial Stores. Today it is home to a car spares business and an estate agent. On the left is Woollatt & Coggin's chemist's shop. This has been a pharmacy since the mid 1700s, when it closed as a public house. It seems that it was originally run by Samuel Parkes Woollatt, who was joined by Coggin to form the partnership.

Ware, The Priory 1925 77114
The Priory was built as a friary for Franciscan Grey Friars in the 14th century. At the Dissolution of the Monasteries, it was given as a private house to Thomas Birch, one of the yeoman of the Crown. In 1685 it was bought by Robert Hadley of Great Munden and eventually passed to Martin Hadsley Gosselin, who carried out major restorations in 1849. In 1913 a Mrs Croft purchased the Priory, and during the Great War offered it as a hospital for convalescing soldiers. After the Great War, it passed to Ware Urban District Council (later Ware Town Council) on a 999-year lease at a rent of three shillings per annum. In 1994 a major renovation programme was carried out by the Priory Trustees.

Ware, New Road 1925 78294
Even before the arrival of the railway, Ware was home to a population of rising middle-class entrepreneurs who demanded the most modern housing. The northern end of New Road, with its spacious up-to-date villas, catered for the shop-owners and factory managers. Four churches were built in the 1800s, including the Wesleyan Methodist church of 1838, Christ Church of 1858 and the Catholic Apostolic church; today there are five. At the south end of New Road were shops, stores and businesses, including F Cutmore, sanitary engineer, decorator and undertaker. During the Second World War, Ware escaped most of the bombing; however, a stick of bombs damaged a number of houses on New Road.

ESTATE
AGENTS
ENFIELD
3226 NO

Ware, High Street c1965 W24072
Looking west along the High Street, one is struck by the minimal amount of traffic. Nonetheless, in 1976 it was necessary to build the Ware by-pass to alleviate congestion in the High Street. The Blue Boot Stores has been replaced by Ingles's furniture store, and Taylors has taken over the responsibilities of Page's Forage Stores in selling pet supplies under the name of Wagger's Food Farm. The gap to the east of the Wine Lodge is filled with an unusual advertising pagoda (right). There had been a building here which was burnt down - the occupier narrowly escaped with his life, but broke his legs when jumping from an upstairs window. The first building on the left was Harradence's department store, which encompassed Nos 65 to 73 High Street. They were agents for Jaeger's 'Gentleman's Sanitary Underwear' - nothing more intriguing than Britain's first cotton 'long johns'.

▼ **Ware, Ware Park Sanitorium 1925** 78298
Ware Park, rebuilt in the 1880s by William Parker, is located about three-quarters of a mile north-west of Bengeo on the outskirts of Hertford. After the Great War, it was used as a sanatorium for TB sufferers; it closed in the 1970s, when it was converted to private residences. In the 1600s, the gardens in the park were renowned as being amongst the most tasteful in England. Sir Henry Wotton, in 1624, said that the scene was 'without parallel among foreign Nationes ... in the Garden of Sir Henry Fanshawe at his seat in Ware-Parke'. In September 1941 a landmine landed in the park, and was examined by the Royal Navy bomb disposal team. It was reported to be safe, but when it arrived in Ware for display, it was found to be warm and ticking. It was quickly taken to the Watton Road Gravel pits and detonated.

▼ **Bengeo, St Leonard's Church 1922** 71877
St Leonard's church at Bengeo, probably the oldest building in the Hertford area, dates from the 12th century. It appears to have been built in 1120 to replace a wooden church, which was probably destroyed by the Danes. There is an anchorite's cell behind the panelling in the north wall, and a fine replacement tiled roof over the semicircular apsidal east end.

▲ **Bengeo, St Leonard's Church 1929** 81779
This fine example of Norman architecture was in a derelict state, and the church of Holy Trinity in New Road, consecrated in June 1855, took over as the place of regular worship. An inappropriate gabled roof had been built over the semicircular apsidal east end. Fortunately the church was restored both externally and internally, and now offers a fine view across the site of the present Gosselin Road.

◄ **Port Hill, From Hartham 1929** 81782

The young girl in her fashionable cloche hat dips for minnows in the River Beane, whilst her friend waits patiently for her turn. In the background are the 'stepped' houses on Port Hill, which leads from Cowbridge up to Bengeo. Port Hill is the steepest in Hertford, and the road was strewn with sand to help the horses drawing the drays to obtain a firm grip. The sand boxes still stood by the side of the road until recent years.

Hertford The Drinking Fountain 1922 71858

In 1888, when the site for the new library at Old Cross was being dug, a jumble of stones from the 13th-century St Mary the Less were uncovered. These were reassembled, rather randomly, in the form of a drinking fountain. The library, which was also home to the Art School, was opened by A J Balfour, who later became Prime Minister.

Hertford, St Andrew's Street 1929 81777

Sad to say, many of the timber-framed buildings in St Andrew's Street were demolished in the 1960s. One of the survivors was the Old Verger's House (right), which was restored around 1893; today it holds the showrooms of Beckwith's Antiques. The building, hidden behind the second gable of the Verger's House was restored too. With additions behind, it became St Nicholas Hall.

Hertford The War Memorial 1922 71855

The war memorial, standing in Parliament Square, was completed in 1921. Designed by Sir Aston Wenn and surmounted by a hart sculpted by Alfred Drury, it is built of Portland stone. A number of buildings had to be demolished to make space for the memorial close to Parliament Row - here, it has been suggested, parliament met in the 1500s during outbreaks of plague in London.

Hertford, The Castle 1922

71856

Only the 15th-century brick gatehouse to the castle survives. In December 1216, the castle was besieged and captured by the army of the French Dauphin. Later it became a gaol for royal prisoners, who included Margaret of Anjou, wife of King Henry VI, King David II of Scotland and King John of France. It became the residence of the Marquis of Devonshire in the late 1880s. Much of the grounds and garden walls were restored in 1912, and the walks were opened to the public.

Hertford, Honey Lane 1933 85543
This narrow lane shows exactly how the back streets of the old town would have looked 200 years ago. The upper faces of the buildings are decorated with ornate plasterwork called pargetting, and the residents on each side could almost shake hands across the street from the windows. Always a busy area of trade, in 1933 Honey Lane boasted a jumble of shops selling household goods, including baskets and crockery.

Hertford, Maidenhead Street and Bull Plain c1950 H77003
Originally known as Back Street, Maidenhead Street was a bustling centre of trade and commerce. Gravesons (left) was erected in late 1890 on the site of an old timber-framed building, and became a focal point on the corner of Salisbury Square. In the gap between the buildings in the centre of the photograph stood shops and offices. These were destroyed by fire on 6 May 1917.

Hertford, The County Hospital 1933 85540c
Originally called the Infirmary, the County Hospital (1908) in North Row was designed by Thomas Smith, later County Surveyor to Hertfordshire (1837-1875), and opened to receive patients in 1833. In fact, Smith designed most of the buildings in North Row, and he lived in North Road House opposite the infirmary. The hospital was always proud of its gardens and grounds. Whilst the lawn is being rolled to perfect smoothness, the post office Morris Commercial van delivers the mail.

Waterford, The Old Windmi Tea Rooms c1960 W291024a
Waterford lies along the North Road from Hertford towards Stapleford and Stevenage - the road follows the course of the meandering River Beane. The row of four whitewashed cottages in the foreground leac up to the Vicarage Lane turning on the right; the lane crosses the river about 200 yards nortl of the Overflow, a weir at Waterford Marsh. Just after the lane stands what was in the 1950s the Old Windmill Tea Rooms - it had been the post office in the 1930s. Today it is private residence.

Hertford, Panshanger 1933 85564

Panshanger was built in 1806 by Peter, fifth Earl Cowper on high ground close to the valley of the River Mimram. In 1855 the mansion narrowly escaped destruction by a fire which caused £12,000 damage. The unique art collection that included works by Rembrandt, Van Dyck, Poussin and Rubens was saved. Eventually, Panshanger passed to Lord Desborough, and when Lady Desborough died in 1955, the mansion was demolished. Only the stables now remain.

Benington, St Peter's Church c1960 B406011

Records suggest that a church stood on this site in the early 9th century. This present building dates from the 13th century. One of the tombs inside the church commemorates the Caesar family, whose most famous member, Julius Caesar, once held the Great Seal of England. He was born Caesar Aldemar, and Queen Mary allowed the family to adopt the name Julius in perpetuity. A fine carving on the tower appears to depict Josef Stalin, but it is actually the likeness of David Warner, one-time sexton.

Walkern, The Church of St Mary the Virgin c1960 W289002

The River Beane runs close to the church, and is liable to heavy flooding. The church stands on a slight mound to the north-east where it is safe from damage, although photographs of flooding show water lapping up against the path leading to the south porch. In 1340 an outbreak of 'murrain', possibly anthrax, made farming impossible and left large areas of land unploughed. Seven years later, the Black Death reached England, and many local people lie buried in the churchyard, victims of this tragic plague. Another tragic figure in the history of Walkern was Jane Wenham, said to be the last woman in England to be prosecuted as a witch.

Walkern, The White, High Street c1960 W289004
The White Lion, one of many public houses in the village, was called the Rose and Crown in 1766, when it formed part of a marriage settlement between Mary Field and John Smith of Hitchin. Although the marriage settlement is the earliest mention of the house, much of the building dates from the 16th century. Around 1800 the name changed to the White Lion. Walkern was well-known for its production of alcoholic and soft drinks. In 1870 the Wright family took advantage of a deep spring well for brewing. They turned to cider in 1924 - the only cider makers in Hertfordshire. By 1955 they made only soft drinks, and they closed in 1980; the factory, at the south end of the village, is now housing.

Walkern, Church End c1960 W289006
Beecroft Lane runs opposite the lane that leads to the church at Church End. In 1410, the rector of Walkern had his hive of bees stolen, along with the honey, by one John Coke - it is said that the hives were kept in Beecroft Lane. Note the Wealden-style house next to the lane, and the interesting country petrol station preparing to serve the visiting Austin. The building is typical of the old coach-building businesses that became garages when motor cars began to replace horse power.

Index

Frith Book Co Titles

www.francisfrith.co.uk

The Frith Book Company publishes over 100 new titles each year. A selection of those currently available are listed below. For latest catalogue please contact Frith Book Co.

Town Books 96 pages, approx 100 photos. County and Themed Books 128 pages, approx 150 photos (unless specified). All titles hardback laminated case and jacket except those indicated pb (paperback)

Amersham, Chesham & Rickmansworth (pb)	1-85937-340-2	£9.99
Ancient Monuments & Stone Circles	1-85937-143-4	£17.99
Aylesbury (pb)	1-85937-227-9	£9.99
Bakewell	1-85937-113-2	£12.99
Barnstaple (pb)	1-85937-300-3	£9.99
Bath (pb)	1-85937419-0	£9.99
Bedford (pb)	1-85937-205-8	£9.99
Berkshire (pb)	1-85937-191-4	£9.99
Berkshire Churches	1-85937-170-1	£17.99
Blackpool (pb)	1-85937-382-8	£9.99
Bognor Regis (pb)	1-85937-431-x	£9.99
Bournemouth	1-85937-067-5	£12.99
Bradford (pb)	1-85937-204-x	£9.99
Brighton & Hove(pb)	1-85937-192-2	£8.99
Bristol (pb)	1-85937-264-3	£9.99
British Life A Century Ago (pb)	1-85937-213-9	£9.99
Buckinghamshire (pb)	1-85937-200-7	£9.99
Camberley (pb)	1-85937-222-8	£9.99
Cambridge (pb)	1-85937-422-0	£9.99
Cambridgeshire (pb)	1-85937-420-4	£9.99
Canals & Waterways (pb)	1-85937-291-0	£9.99
Canterbury Cathedral (pb)	1-85937-179-5	£9.99
Cardiff (pb)	1-85937-093-4	£9.99
Carmarthenshire	1-85937-216-3	£14.99
Chelmsford (pb)	1-85937-310-0	£9.99
Cheltenham (pb)	1-85937-095-0	£9.99
Cheshire (pb)	1-85937-271-6	£9.99
Chester	1-85937-090-x	£12.99
Chesterfield	1-85937-378-x	£9.99
Chichester (pb)	1-85937-228-7	£9.99
Colchester (pb)	1-85937-188-4	£8.99
Cornish Coast	1-85937-163-9	£14.99
Cornwall (pb)	1-85937-229-5	£9.99
Cornwall Living Memories	1-85937-248-1	£14.99
Cotswolds (pb)	1-85937-230-9	£9.99
Cotswolds Living Memories	1-85937-255-4	£14.99
County Durham	1-85937-123-x	£14.99
Croydon Living Memories	1-85937-162-0	£9.99
Cumbria	1-85937-101-9	£14.99
Dartmoor	1-85937-145-0	£14.99
Derby (pb)	1-85937-367-4	£9.99
Derbyshire (pb)	1-85937-196-5	£9.99
Devon (pb)	1-85937-297-x	£9.99
Dorset (pb)	1-85937-269-4	£9.99
Dorset Churches	1-85937-172-8	£17.99
Dorset Coast (pb)	1-85937-299-6	£9.99
Dorset Living Memories	1-85937-210-4	£14.99
Down the Severn	1-85937-118-3	£14.99
Down the Thames (pb)	1-85937-278-3	£9.99
Down the Trent	1-85937-311-9	£14.99
Dublin (pb)	1-85937-231-7	£9.99
East Anglia (pb)	1-85937-265-1	£9.99
East London	1-85937-080-2	£14.99
East Sussex	1-85937-130-2	£14.99
Eastbourne	1-85937-061-6	£12.99
Edinburgh (pb)	1-85937-193-0	£8.99
England in the 1880s	1-85937-331-3	£17.99
English Castles (pb)	1-85937-434-4	£9.99
English Country Houses	1-85937-161-2	£17.99
Essex (pb)	1-85937-270-8	£9.99
Exeter	1-85937-126-4	£12.99
Exmoor	1-85937-132-9	£14.99
Falmouth	1-85937-066-7	£12.99
Folkestone (pb)	1-85937-124-8	£9.99
Glasgow (pb)	1-85937-190-6	£9.99
Gloucestershire	1-85937-102-7	£14.99
Great Yarmouth (pb)	1-85937-426-3	£9.99
Greater Manchester (pb)	1-85937-266-x	£9.99
Guildford (pb)	1-85937-410-7	£9.99
Hampshire (pb)	1-85937-279-1	£9.99
Hampshire Churches (pb)	1-85937-207-4	£9.99
Harrogate	1-85937-423-9	£9.99
Hastings & Bexhill (pb)	1-85937-131-0	£9.99
Heart of Lancashire (pb)	1-85937-197-3	£9.99
Helston (pb)	1-85937-214-7	£9.99
Hereford (pb)	1-85937-175-2	£9.99
Herefordshire	1-85937-174-4	£14.99
Hertfordshire (pb)	1-85937-247-3	£9.99
Horsham (pb)	1-85937-432-8	£9.99
Humberside	1-85937-215-5	£14.99
Hythe, Romney Marsh & Ashford	1-85937-256-2	£9.99

Available from your local bookshop or from the publisher

Frith Book Co Titles (continued)

Ipswich (pb)	1-85937-424-7	£9.99
Ireland (pb)	1-85937-181-7	£9.99
Isle of Man (pb)	1-85937-268-6	£9.99
Isles of Scilly	1-85937-136-1	£14.99
Isle of Wight (pb)	1-85937-429-8	£9.99
Isle of Wight Living Memories	1-85937-304-6	£14.99
Kent (pb)	1-85937-189-2	£9.99
Kent Living Memories	1-85937-125-6	£14.99
Lake District (pb)	1-85937-275-9	£9.99
Lancaster, Morecambe & Heysham (pb)	1-85937-233-3	£9.99
Leeds (pb)	1-85937-202-3	£9.99
Leicester	1-85937-073-x	£12.99
Leicestershire (pb)	1-85937-185-x	£9.99
Lincolnshire (pb)	1-85937-433-6	£9.99
Liverpool & Merseyside (pb)	1-85937-234-1	£9.99
London (pb)	1-85937-183-3	£9.99
Ludlow (pb)	1-85937-176-0	£9.99
Luton (pb)	1-85937-235-x	£9.99
Maidstone	1-85937-056-x	£14.99
Manchester (pb)	1-85937-198-1	£9.99
Middlesex	1-85937-158-2	£14.99
New Forest	1-85937-128-0	£14.99
Newark (pb)	1-85937-366-6	£9.99
Newport, Wales (pb)	1-85937-258-9	£9.99
Newquay (pb)	1-85937-421-2	£9.99
Norfolk (pb)	1-85937-195-7	£9.99
Norfolk Living Memories	1-85937-217-1	£14.99
Northamptonshire	1-85937-150-7	£14.99
Northumberland Tyne & Wear (pb)	1-85937-281-3	£9.99
North Devon Coast	1-85937-146-9	£14.99
North Devon Living Memories	1-85937-261-9	£14.99
North London	1-85937-206-6	£14.99
North Wales (pb)	1-85937-298-8	£9.99
North Yorkshire (pb)	1-85937-236-8	£9.99
Norwich (pb)	1-85937-194-9	£8.99
Nottingham (pb)	1-85937-324-0	£9.99
Nottinghamshire (pb)	1-85937-187-6	£9.99
Oxford (pb)	1-85937-411-5	£9.99
Oxfordshire (pb)	1-85937-430-1	£9.99
Peak District (pb)	1-85937-280-5	£9.99
Penzance	1-85937-069-1	£12.99
Peterborough (pb)	1-85937-219-8	£9.99
Piers	1-85937-237-6	£17.99
Plymouth	1-85937-119-1	£12.99
Poole & Sandbanks (pb)	1-85937-251-1	£9.99
Preston (pb)	1-85937-212-0	£9.99
Reading (pb)	1-85937-238-4	£9.99
Romford (pb)	1-85937-319-4	£9.99
Salisbury (pb)	1-85937-239-2	£9.99
Scarborough (pb)	1-85937-379-8	£9.99
St Albans (pb)	1-85937-341-0	£9.99
St Ives (pb)	1-85937415-8	£9.99
Scotland (pb)	1-85937-182-5	£9.99
Scottish Castles (pb)	1-85937-323-2	£9.99
Sevenoaks & Tunbridge	1-85937-057-8	£12.99
Sheffield, South Yorks (pb)	1-85937-267-8	£9.99
Shrewsbury (pb)	1-85937-325-9	£9.99
Shropshire (pb)	1-85937-326-7	£9.99
Somerset	1-85937-153-1	£14.99
South Devon Coast	1-85937-107-8	£14.99
South Devon Living Memories	1-85937-168-x	£14.99
South Hams	1-85937-220-1	£14.99
Southampton (pb)	1-85937-427-1	£9.99
Southport (pb)	1-85937-425-5	£9.99
Staffordshire	1-85937-047-0	£12.99
Stratford upon Avon	1-85937-098-5	£12.99
Suffolk (pb)	1-85937-221-x	£9.99
Suffolk Coast	1-85937-259-7	£14.99
Surrey (pb)	1-85937-240-6	£9.99
Sussex (pb)	1-85937-184-1	£9.99
Swansea (pb)	1-85937-167-1	£9.99
Tees Valley & Cleveland	1-85937-211-2	£14.99
Thanet (pb)	1-85937-116-7	£9.99
Tiverton (pb)	1-85937-178-7	£9.99
Torbay	1-85937-063-2	£12.99
Truro	1-85937-147-7	£12.99
Victorian and Edwardian Cornwall	1-85937-252-x	£14.99
Victorian & Edwardian Devon	1-85937-253-8	£14.99
Victorian & Edwardian Kent	1-85937-149-3	£14.99
Vic & Ed Maritime Album	1-85937-144-2	£17.99
Victorian and Edwardian Sussex	1-85937-157-4	£14.99
Victorian & Edwardian Yorkshire	1-85937-154-x	£14.99
Victorian Seaside	1-85937-159-0	£17.99
Villages of Devon (pb)	1-85937-293-7	£9.99
Villages of Kent (pb)	1-85937-294-5	£9.99
Villages of Sussex (pb)	1-85937-295-3	£9.99
Warwickshire (pb)	1-85937-203-1	£9.99
Welsh Castles (pb)	1-85937-322-4	£9.99
West Midlands (pb)	1-85937-289-9	£9.99
West Sussex	1-85937-148-5	£14.99
West Yorkshire (pb)	1-85937-201-5	£9.99
Weymouth (pb)	1-85937-209-0	£9.99
Wiltshire (pb)	1-85937-277-5	£9.99
Wiltshire Churches (pb)	1-85937-171-x	£9.99
Wiltshire Living Memories	1-85937-245-7	£14.99
Winchester (pb)	1-85937-428-x	£9.99
Windmills & Watermills	1-85937-242-2	£17.99
Worcester (pb)	1-85937-165-5	£9.99
Worcestershire	1-85937-152-3	£14.99
York (pb)	1-85937-199-x	£9.99
Yorkshire (pb)	1-85937-186-8	£9.99
Yorkshire Living Memories	1-85937-166-3	£14.99

See Frith books on the internet www.francisfrith.co.uk

FRITH PRODUCTS & SERVICES

Francis Frith would doubtless be pleased to know that the pioneering publishing venture he started in 1860 still continues today. A hundred and forty years later, The Francis Frith Collection continues in the same innovative tradition and is now one of the foremost publishers of vintage photographs in the world. Some of the current activities include:

Interior Decoration

Today Frith's photographs can be seen framed and as giant wall murals in thousands of pubs, restaurants, hotels, banks, retail stores and other public buildings throughout the country. In every case they enhance the unique local atmosphere of the places they depict and provide reminders of gentler days in an increasingly busy and frenetic world.

Product Promotions

Frith products are used by many major companies to promote the sales of their own products or to reinforce their own history and heritage. Frith promotions have been used by Hovis bread, Courage beers, Scots Porage Oats, Colman's mustard, Cadbury's foods, Mellow Birds coffee, Dunhill pipe tobacco, Guinness, and Bulmer's Cider.

Genealogy and Family History

As the interest in family history and roots grows world-wide, more and more people are turning to Frith's photographs of Great Britain for images of the towns, villages and streets where their ancestors lived; and, of course, photographs of the churches and chapels where their ancestors were christened, married and buried are an essential part of every genealogy tree and family album.

Frith Products

All Frith photographs are available Framed or just as Mounted Prints and Posters (size 23 x 16 inches). These may be ordered from the address below. From time to time other products - Address Books, Calendars, Table Mats, etc - are available.

The Internet

Already twenty thousand Frith photographs can be viewed and purchased on the internet through the Frith websites and a myriad of partner sites.

For more detailed information on Frith companies and products, look at these sites:

www.francisfrith.co.uk
www.francisfrith.com
(for North American visitors)

See the complete list of Frith Books at:
www.francisfrith.co.uk

This web site is regularly updated with the latest list of publications from the Frith Book Company. If you wish to buy books relating to another part of the country that your local bookshop does not stock, you may purchase on-line.

For further information, trade, or author enquiries please contact us at the address below:

The Francis Frith Collection, Frith's Barn, Teffont, Salisbury, Wiltshire, England SP3 5QP.
Tel: +44 (0)1722 716 376 Fax: +44 (0)1722 716 881 Email: sales@francisfrith.co.uk

See Frith books on the internet www.francisfrith.co.uk

TO RECEIVE YOUR FREE MOUNTED PRINT

Mounted Print
Overall size 14 x 11 inches

Cut out this Voucher and return it with your remittance for £2.25 to cover postage and handling, to UK addresses. For overseas addresses please include £4.00 post and handling. Choose any photograph included in this book. Your SEPIA print will be A4 in size, and mounted in a cream mount with burgundy rule line, overall size 14 x 11 inches.

Order additional Mounted Prints at HALF PRICE (only £7.49 each*)
If there are further pictures you would like to order, possibly as gifts for friends and family, purchase them at half price (no additional postage and handling required).

Have your Mounted Prints framed*
For an additional £14.95 per print you can have your chosen Mounted Print framed in an elegant polished wood and gilt moulding, overall size 16 x 13 inches (no additional postage and handling required).

*** IMPORTANT!**
These special prices are only available if ordered using the original voucher on this page (no copies permitted) and at the same time as your free Mounted Print, for delivery to the same address

Frith Collectors' Guild

From time to time we publish a magazine of news and stories about Frith photographs and further special offers of Frith products. If you would like 12 months FREE membership, please return this form.

Send completed forms to:
The Francis Frith Collection, Frith's Barn, Teffont, Salisbury, Wiltshire SP3 5QP

Voucher for **FREE** and Reduced Price Frith Prints

Picture no.	Page number	Qty	Mounted @ £7.49	Framed + £14.95	Total Cost
		1	**Free of charge***	£	£
			£7.49	£	£
			£7.49	£	£
			£7.49	£	£
			£7.49	£	£
			£7.49	£	£
Please allow 28 days for delivery			*** Post & handling**		**£2.25**
Book Title			**Total Order Cost**		**£**

Please do not photocopy this voucher. Only the original is valid, so please cut it out and return it to us.

I enclose a cheque / postal order for £ ....
made payable to 'The Francis Frith Collection'
OR please debit my Mastercard / Visa / Switch / Amex card
(credit cards please on all overseas orders)

Number ....

Issue No (Switch only) .... Valid from (Amex/Switch) ....

Expires .... Signature ....

Name Mr/Mrs/Ms ....

Address ....

....

....

Postcode .... Daytime Tel No ....

Email Address ....

Valid to 31/12/04

The Francis Frith Collectors' Guild

Please enrol me as a member for 12 months free of charge.

Name Mr/Mrs/Ms ....

Address ....

....

....

.... Postcode ....

Free Print - see overleaf

Would you like to find out more about Francis Frith?

We have recently recruited some entertaining speakers who are happy to visit local groups, clubs and societies to give an illustrated talk documenting Frith's travels and photographs. If you are a member of such a group and are interested in hosting a presentation, we would love to hear from you.

Our speakers bring with them a small selection of our local town and county books, together with sample prints. They are happy to take orders. A small proportion of the order value is donated to the group who have hosted the presentation. The talks are therefore an excellent way of fundraising for small groups and societies.

Can you help us with information about any of the Frith photographs in this book?

We are gradually compiling an historical record for each of the photographs in the Frith archive. It is always fascinating to find out the names of the people shown in the pictures, as well as insights into the shops, buildings and other features depicted.

If you recognize anyone in the photographs in this book, or if you have information not already included in the author's caption, do let us know. We would love to hear from you, and will try to publish it in future books or articles.

Our production team

Frith books are produced by a small dedicated team at offices in the converted Grade II listed 18th-century barn at Teffont near Salisbury, illustrated above. Most have worked with the Frith Collection for many years. All have in common one quality: they have a passion for the Frith Collection. The team is constantly expanding, but currently includes:

Jason Buck, John Buck, Douglas Burns, Ruth Butler, Heather Crisp, Isobel Hall, Hazel Heaton, Peter Horne, James Kinnear, Tina Leary, Hannah Marsh, Sue Molloy, Kate Rotondetto, Dean Scource, Eliza Sackett, Terence Sackett, Sandra Sanger, Lewis Taylor, Shelley Tolcher, Clive Wathen and Jenny Wathen.